Plentiful Harvest: Fertile Ground

Marlowe R. Scott

Plentiful Harvest
Fertile Ground

Marlowe R. Scott

Pearly Gates Publishing LLC
INSPIRING CHRISTIAN AUTHORS TO BE AUTHORS
Pearly Gates Publishing, LLC, Houston, Texas

Plentiful Harvest: Fertile Ground

Plentiful Harvest: Fertile Ground

Copyright © 2018
Marlowe R. Scott

All Rights Reserved.
No portion of this publication may be reproduced, stored in any electronic system, or transmitted in any form or by any means (electronic, mechanical, photocopy, recording, or otherwise) without written permission from the publisher or author. Brief quotations may be used in literary reviews.

ISBN 13: 978-1-947445-37-6
Library of Congress Control Number: 2018959939

Scripture references are taken from the King James Version (KJV) of the Holy Bible and used with permission from Zondervan via Biblegateway.com. Public Domain.

For information and bulk ordering, contact:
Pearly Gates Publishing, LLC
Angela Edwards, CEO
P.O. Box 62287
Houston, TX 77205
BestSeller@PearlyGatesPublishing.com

Marlowe R. Scott

Dedication

To the Farmers of the world who toil, plant, and give us food for our daily bread. Their diligence through unpredictable seasons, pestilence, and climate changes **NEED** to be and **MUST** be applauded, praised, and appreciated!

Thank you!

Acknowledgements

First, to God for giving me His leading and Holy Word, and the inspiration and ability to witness to others through writing Christ-Centered books.

Secondly, to my Christian parents, Carl and Helena Harris, who loved me, encouraged me, and planted many life-sustaining seeds which have kept me through the years and storms of life.

Thirdly, to my gifted daughter, Angela R. Edwards, the Publisher of all my writings through her Christian publishing company, Pearly Gates Publishing, LLC of Houston, Texas. She has supported and guided each book in ways too numerous to mention.

Marlowe R. Scott

Preface

Inspiration and concept for this book began with remembering the numbers of youth I had taught in Sunday School church classes and related activities, such as conferences and choirs.

Positive seeds of love, responsibility, sharing, kindness to others, as well as respect fell into their lives while they were taught by me. This equated to planting, nurturing, and growing those seeds in fertile ground.

Many of those youth have developed into fine examples of Christians who are Christ-centered and active in their churches, communities, and businesses. We still keep in touch, primarily through social media. Their inner-man/inner-woman were definitely enriched and they are producing an abundant harvest for now and years to come.

Praise and thank God for the increase!

Plentiful Harvest: Fertile Ground

Introduction

Should a theme scripture be chosen for *Plentiful Harvest: Fertile Ground*, it would be David's prayer in Psalm 17:8:

*"Keep me as the apple of the eye;
hide me under the shadow of thy wings."*

Additional scripture references are found in:

- Deuteronomy 32:10 – *"...He led him about, He instructed Him, He kept him as the apple of His eye."*
- Proverbs 7:2 – *"Keep my commandments and live; and my law as the apple of thine eye."*
- Zechariah 2:8 – *"...for he that toucheth you toucheth the apple of His eye."*

As with my other inspired publications, an agricultural theme and analogies are interspersed throughout this book.

Pearly Gates Publishing's CEO, Angela Edwards, reminds us, **"MY Words Have Power!"** For those who have read my previous books, I apologize in advance if some things are repeated. Prayerfully, the words herein make a powerful difference in your life and those you touch.

Marlowe R. Scott

As you read, you will find verses of hymns, an inspired poem, and questions to answer regarding your "seed-planting" in others. Some of the hymns may ring a familiar memory to older Christians. At the same time, younger readers and newer converts will have insight into the message of hymns no longer used in many worship services today.

There is a story shared in this book about a Christian apple seed planter known as Johnny Appleseed, as well as information regarding the bountiful benefits of God's fruit: the apple.

The pictures of a cornucopia throughout the book represent a plentiful harvest (usually gathered in the Fall) of beautiful, nourishing apples. Cornucopias may also display a mixture of fruit and vegetables.

Enjoy—and why not eat an apple while reading? It may just "keep the doctor away"…as the saying goes!

Plentiful Harvest: Fertile Ground

TABLE OF CONTENTS

Dedication	vi
Acknowledgements	vii
Preface	viii
Introduction	ix
Apple of God's Eye	1
Planting in Fertile Grounds	2
The Apple — God's Fruit Gem	7
I've Got a Testimony!	18
Johnny Appleseed	20
The Revived Desert	25
Conclusion	26
Prayer	28
About the Author	29
Glossary	32
Hymns Reference	33
Amazon Best-Selling Books Written By Marlowe R. Scott	34

Marlowe R. Scott

Plentiful Harvest!

Plentiful Harvest: Fertile Ground

Apple of God's Eye

The psalmist David prayed a beautiful message in Psalm 17:8—the theme scripture. For those who love and appreciate poetry as I do, I highly recommend you search "Apple of God's Eye Poems" on the internet. They are beautiful and inspiring!

Following is my poetic rendition sharing the value of the Apple of God's Eye to me.

The Apple of God's Eye
By Marlowe R. Scott © 2018

My God keeps me as the Apple of His Eye.
He hides me under the shadow of angel's wings.
He prepares the way for me each day
As my soul rejoices and sings.

My God blesses me with the Holy Spirit
Because He knows my needs and thoughts;
God gave me talents and spiritual gifts
To serve mankind as every Christian ought.

I must encourage and bless children, women, and men
By showing God's love to those met along the way.
One day, His Son Jesus Christ will come for me
And I'll go to Heaven praising and singing all day.

You see, being the Apple of God's Eye
Assures He is always close; this I know.
You are invited to join me on this heavenly journey
Where all God's converted children go.

Marlowe R. Scott

Planting in Fertile Grounds

When my children were young, I ensured we regularly went to Sunday School and church. As they were in their classes, I taught Sunday School, helped with the young people's department, and attended church school activities and conferences. At those times, I did not realize that many "seeds" of kindness, love, and genuine concern had been planted and that those seeds were still growing and producing "fruits."

In my first book, *Spiritual Growth: From Milk to Strong Meat*, there is a brief overview of an Apologetics class I took. The class focused on planting seeds in the unsaved or others who needed to be saved and learn how to witness to others. The goal was to nudge others to want to know more about Jesus Christ in a non-critical judgmental manner.

Now, I have been seeing many of the young children I taught in Sunday School and other Christian youth groups blossom into ministers, preachers, and teachers of God's Word, to include Christian publishers and authors of books. They are active in their communities throughout the world! Some have become physicians, engineers, Gospel recording artists, publishers, poets, radio show hosts, and mentors to others. It is

Plentiful Harvest: Fertile Ground

humbling and awesome to think seeds planted years ago are still flourishing.

There was an occasion in 2017 when many of the former youth (now men and women) had gathered. Each one saw me and immediately came to give me a smile, hug, and kiss on the cheek!!!

Eventually, an older woman came over to me, introduced herself, and asked me, *"Who are you?"* I was stunned briefly and told her my name. She shared that she noticed many people — including the young men and women — come to me. I told her my daughter was among the group and, as the youth grew up in church, I worked with them.

The same reaction of people being drawn to me has also occurred in other settings, to include churches, social affairs, and even when I was working. I am thankful and praise God that He has blessed me with spiritual gifts and qualities to reach others and further increase His Kingdom.

Marlowe R. Scott

Journaling Questions

1. Where have you planted "seeds" in others?

_____
_____
_____
_____
_____
_____
_____
_____
_____
_____
_____
_____
_____
_____
_____
_____

Plentiful Harvest: Fertile Ground

2. How have those "seeds" you planted developed?

_____
_____
_____
_____
_____
_____
_____
_____
_____
_____
_____
_____
_____
_____
_____
_____
_____
_____
_____

3. What special care did you give to ensure your "seeds" were ready for the harvest of life and, ultimately, Heaven?

_____
_____
_____
_____
_____
_____
_____
_____
_____
_____
_____
_____
_____
_____
_____
_____
_____

Plentiful Harvest: Fertile Ground

The Apple—God's Fruit Gem

God created a perfect world thousands of years go. Part of the many tree species include the apple tree. It is definitely worthy of being the focus and theme of the title of this book. The apple tree is plentiful, yielding a great harvest. It thrives in fertile ground and produces prolifically. Because God created healthy foods for man to eat, in considering the apple, it must be given lots of credit for being a "gem" of a fruit.

Before going further, I must interject something about Adam and Eve in the Garden of Eden. Genesis 2:16-17 speaks of the Tree of the Knowledge of Good and Evil. God told Adam not to eat of it or he would surely die. The Bible then tells of Eve being tempted to eat the fruit by the devil and then offering the fruit for Adam to also eat of the forbidden fruit. Nowhere does the **BIBLE** say is was an *APPLE*! God created many different fruit trees. Over the years (and when I was a child), children's storybooks showed Eve with a red apple being tempted by Satan. Theatrical productions have also depicted this fallacy. The point is that Adam and Eve disobeyed God's command and the apple may have gotten a bad reputation.

In actuality, the apple is a "star" in the fruit family! Should you cut an apple across its middle (rather than from the stem downward), you will see a star with seeds inside! I personally was amazed at that fact — something I never noticed before.

It is easy to associate an apple's star core with the creation of the heavens. Jesus was also referred to as a 'Star' in the Bible. He was called the 'Star of David' and 'Seed of Abraham.'

Plentiful Harvest: Fertile Ground

Luke 8 records Jesus' parable about a sower of seeds. In verse 11, Jesus says, *"Now the parable is this: The seed is the Word of God."* As the Word of God nourishes our spiritual life, so the apple nourishes our physical body.

Not only is the apple tree a prolific, long-lived tree, it is nutritious and versatile in its use. Countless trees can be started by either seeds or root stock. It may produce apples on the average of 15 to 40 years, depending on variety and care. There is documentation of trees producing 100 years! The average harvest is 30 bushels a year per tree in orchards, and one bushel may weigh 42 pounds.

The benefits are too numerous to mention. The following list will convince any and all to eat more apples:

- ❖ Aids in whiter, healthier teeth
- ❖ Avoiding Alzheimer's
- ❖ Protection from Parkinson's
- ❖ Defender / Curbs cancers
- ❖ Decrease diabetes
- ❖ Lowers cholesterol
- ❖ Stronger, healthier heart
- ❖ Strengthen immune system

- ❖ Reduce strokes
- ❖ Boosts brain health
- ❖ Treats anemia

The apple is also renown for tasty food dishes such as:
- ❖ Pies
- ❖ Dumplings
- ❖ Cakes
- ❖ Apple sauce
- ❖ Jelly
- ❖ Sliced and used with cheese or peanut butter as a snack
- ❖ Juice
- ❖ Cider

The plentiful harvest is found in scriptures and was addressed by Jesus to the disciples. One example is found in Matthew 9:37-38:

"Then saith He unto His disciples, 'The harvest truly is plenteous, but the labourers are few; Pray ye, therefore, the Lord of the harvest, that He will send forth labourers into His harvest."

Plentiful Harvest: Fertile Ground

Another example is found when Jesus appointed 70 and sent them in pairs into the cities before Him. Luke 10:2 beautifully states, *"The harvest is truly great, but the labourers are few; pray ye, therefore, the Lord of the harvest, that He would send forth labourers into His harvest."*

In years past, the tradition was to have in the home during the Thanksgiving season a centerpiece on the table or sideboard, a cornucopia filled with the fruits and vegetables of the season. Today, the yearly Thanksgiving parades often have floats with pilgrims and a large cornucopia filled with assorted fruits and vegetables.

Marlowe R. Scott

The following hymn was sung yearly in my church when I was growing up. It was during Thanksgiving season, as well as during the annual harvest of crops placed at the altar and we praised God for the bountiful vegetables and fruits produced.

"Come, Ye Thankful People, Come" by Henry Alford

Come, ye thankful people, come!
All the world is God's own field,
Fruit unto His praise to yield;
Wheat and tares together sown,
Unto joy or sorrow grown;
First the blade, and then the ear,
Then the full corn shall appear:
Lord of harvest, great that we
Wholesome grain and pure may be.

Plentiful Harvest: Fertile Ground

I pause in writing because it is imperative to note that today's times are not always planting productive seeds. The list continually grows and changes about the challenges young and old alike are facing. Sadly, I must say it does not always hold true that it takes a village to rear a child. Today's "village" environment may present ever-increasing dangers for our children to include:

- ❖ Molesters
- ❖ Bullying
- ❖ Weapons
- ❖ Gangs
- ❖ Social media
- ❖ False religions
- ❖ Predators

Some false religions, cults, gangs, and even families teach unhealthy habits, satanic rituals, and practice other beliefs, which are sure to lead to eternal damnation. In direct contrast, one church's Mission Statement includes the term 'village', but CHRIST-CENTERED precedes the word village. That makes a great difference!

Government and mankind cannot fix the situation alone. As another song says, *"Jesus is the answer for the world today…"* Saved, committed Christians must stand up, be counted, and heard before the approaching Judgment Day comes!

Plentiful Harvest: Fertile Ground

Journaling Questions

1. How have you supported the "village" concept and influenced others to do so?

_____
_____
_____
_____
_____
_____
_____
_____
_____
_____
_____
_____
_____
_____
_____
_____
_____

2. What value are you adding to the "village" in your neighborhood, workplace, school, church, family, etc.?

_____
_____
_____
_____
_____
_____
_____
_____
_____
_____
_____
_____
_____
_____
_____
_____

Plentiful Harvest: Fertile Ground

3. What are you doing to nourish and keep fertile ground for future generations?

_____
_____
_____
_____
_____
_____
_____
_____
_____
_____
_____
_____
_____
_____
_____
_____
_____

Marlowe R. Scott

I've Got a Testimony!

Rev. Clay Evans sings an uplifting praise song that has been enjoyed for many years. It is appropriate for me as my life's testimony. The simple words are:

"When I look back over my life and I think things over, I can truly say that I've been blessed! I've got a testimony!"

As a federal employee, I once had a business card with a motto that read, **"One Person Can Make A Difference."** I did not know at that time that motto would reap an abundant harvest for me and others. The organization I was employed by had an unfavorable reputation. By using written communication, giving speeches, interacting with the installation's community on a regular basis, and listening to issues critical to the community, the image improved. The complaints decreased, the employees' morale went up, and the directorate and installation won an award recognizing it for overall improvement at the Army Command level!

Plentiful Harvest: Fertile Ground

Just to think: Little me was involved in all of that! But you know the one person who made and is still making a large and far-reaching difference?

Jesus Christ!

Marlowe R. Scott

Johnny Appleseed

Earlier, Johnny Appleseed was mentioned in the Introduction. I learned much about him, and am sharing so you will also learn and enjoy.

While preparing and searching for information to include in this book, the name 'Johnny Appleseed' flashed in my mind. A quick search on the internet found an interesting article written by Kristy Puchko, dated September 26, 2017, which enlightened me.

As a child, I knew the name Johnny Appleseed—his birth name was John Chapman—was in storybooks and was a legendary person. But, like many legends, he was based on an actual person. Johnny was a folk hero and pioneer born in Leominster, Massachusetts on September 26, 1774. He grew up during the Revolutionary War and, while growing up, belonged to the Church of Swedenburg (also known as The New Church that was established in 1787). The church forbade its members from harming God's creation. Therefore, it is easily understood that Johnny was a vocal animal rights activist and vegetarian.

Plentiful Harvest: Fertile Ground

He was known to move west ahead of new settlements and planted apple seeds. Johnny planted seeds because he felt that the grafting process hurt the trees.

The seeds he planted were from tart apples, ideal for hard cider and a drink known as "Applejack." During Prohibition, FBI agents cut down apple orchards that Johnny planted in order to prevent people from making hard cider and hooch (a cheap whiskey).

Over the course of time and due to climate and soil differences, other varieties of apples developed that were suitable for applesauce and baking. Today's farmers and scientists have developed hybrid apples.

In Nova, Ohio, there is an apple tree planted by Johnny that is documented to be over 175 years old! I'm saddened to say that new starts from the tree have been taken by grafting, which is directly contrary to Johnny's Christian beliefs about caring for and respecting God's creation.

Johnny Appleseed (John Chapman) died March 18, 1845. 'National Johnny Appleseed Day' is September 26th and is acknowledged yearly in the United States.

Journaling Questions

1. What have you personally planted to harvest for now and future generations?

_____
_____
_____
_____
_____
_____
_____
_____
_____
_____
_____
_____
_____
_____
_____

Plentiful Harvest: Fertile Ground

2. Are you ready for the harvest? Why or why not?

_____
_____
_____
_____
_____
_____
_____
_____
_____
_____
_____
_____
_____
_____
_____
_____
_____
_____
_____
_____
_____
_____
_____
_____

3. What personal testimony do you have to know you have made a difference in the outcome of the coming harvest?

___

The Revived Desert

There is a story of a dry desert that, for years, bore only stubby plants and cacti. With the climate change, rains came and what appeared to be dead sprang to life with beautiful flowers! The dormant seeds needed life-giving water. This shows it is never too late to blossom. What appears to be dead can live again! There may, however, be long, dry seasons while waiting.

The prophet Isaiah addresses this type of event:

Isaiah 35:6-7 – *"...for in the wilderness shall waters break out, and streams in the desert. And the parched ground shall become a pool, and the thirsty land springs of water..."*

Don't become discouraged when your seed-planting doesn't flourish in your time. Just keep planting and in God's time, the harvest **WILL** come!

Conclusion

As *Plentiful Harvest: Fertile Ground* was read, prayerfully the story and examples ignited a desire for you to recognize and find ways to plant your seeds of love, faith, compassion, spiritual gifts, and talents as you meet and interact with others.

While my experiences of seed-planting and harvesting may be different than yours, everyone has the ability and responsibility to show Christ and sow seeds in others through your character, words, touch, and actions. It has been said many times that sometimes, the only Christ some people see is through **YOU**! You may not see the seed through to harvest time; however, Jesus knows and you will be blessed!

Plentiful Harvest: Fertile Ground

The following hymn, *"Lord of the Living Harvest"* by John S.B. Monsell, illustrates this concept very well:

Lord of the living harvest
That whitens o'er the plain,
Where angels soon shall gather
Their sheaves of golden grain;
Accept these hands of labor,
These hearts to trust and love,
And *deign with them to hasten
Thy kingdom from above.

*Deign – to lower oneself to do something.

Be a seed-planter and blessing to future generations. As it is stated in Psalm 103:17, *"But the mercy of the Lord is from everlasting to everlasting upon them that fear Him, and His righteousness until children's children."*

Marlowe R. Scott

Prayer

Lord Jesus, Son of the Living God,

My prayer once again is that the readers are nourished and encouraged through the reading and application of the messages You have given me. I ask that never-ending blessings are upon each seed-planter so that Your harvest becomes ever-plentiful.

Amen

About the Author

Marlowe R. Scott was born at home in a small, South Jersey community of Cedarville, New Jersey. Her parents were Carl and Helena Harris. Marlowe is a true country girl who loves nature—God's wondrous creation. She enjoys seeing birds preparing nests, wild turkeys roaming the backyard with their young, and the stately deer in the field and property tree line where she lives in Browns Mills, New Jersey.

Marlowe has been blessed with many talents. They include writing, poetry, music, sewing, crocheting, quilting, and floral designs. Her educational focus was the Communication Arts Degree program at Burlington County College, as well as attendance and participation in numerous government-sponsored training venues.

Marlowe's extensive career experiences encompassed duties as Leadership, Education, and Development Facilitator; Equal Employment Opportunity Counselor; Quality Management Facilitator; and member of the New Jersey Quality Board of Examiners. With her commitment to quality, she also participated in video conferences, workshops, and community volunteer activities.

Marlowe R. Scott

One highlight of her career was a conference held in Baltimore, Maryland where she was a member of a select group of individuals who met and interacted with Retired U.S. Army General and Former U.S. Secretary of State, Colin Powell. Marlowe retired after 33 years of dedicated federal civil service.

She has taught Floral Arts and Crafts in adult education, won ribbons for her creative designs, and appeared on television. Currently, she devotes most of her time to quilting and developing her home-based business, M.R.S. Inspirations, with the motto "Magnificent Revelations Are My Specialty." Her creations are focused on making special memories in lap quilts, throws, baby quilts, and pillows which show love and give comfort to the recipient.

Readers of her books have verbally expressed, as well as given written endorsements and testimonies, sharing how they were inspired, experienced spiritual growth, and comfort through her writing and poems. She also received commendation from Former U.S. President Barack Obama and family for sharing with them her book, *Spiritual Growth: From Milk to Strong Meat*.

Plentiful Harvest: Fertile Ground

Marlowe is married to Andrew Scott and has three children: Carl, James, and Angela, as well as five grandchildren and a host of great-grandchildren. She is currently a member of Tabernacle Baptist Church, Burlington, New Jersey.

Glossary

CORNUCOPIA – A curved, hollow goat's horn or similar-shaped receptacle, such as a basket, that is overflowing with fruit and/or vegetables used for decoration symbolizing abundance. Also called "Horn of Plenty."

EQUATED – To be the same or equal.

FALLICY – Mistaken belief; error; misleading.

FERTILE – Capable of producing abundant crops; high-yielding; productive; produce seeds or young.

GRAFTING - The process of joining two plants together (an upper portion and a lower portion) to grow as one stronger plant.

GROUND – Surface of earth; land; land of specified kind; soil/dirt/loam/sod; territory.

HARVEST – Gather crop; reaping; collecting; bring in.

PESTILENCE – Disease that causes people to die; something that is destructive.

PLENTIFUL – Yielding great quantities; abundant; profuse; lavish; generous; prolific.

PREDATOR – Animal or person that hurts, kills, hunts, injures.

PROLIFIC – Much; many; plentiful.

SIDEBOARD - a piece of furniture with drawers, placed along a wall and used for storing dishes.

Hymns Reference

Baton & Mains, Jennings & Graham, Smith & Lamar. (1905). The Methodist Hymnal. The Methodists Book Concern, New York. Cincinnati. Chicago.

Amazon Best-Selling Books Written By Marlowe R. Scott

All titles are available on Amazon and other online retailers.

Plentiful Harvest: Fertile Ground

*Spiritual Growth:
From Milk to Strong Meat*
© 2015

SYNOPSIS:

Spiritual Growth: From Milk to Strong Meat creatively progresses from childhood to the senior life of the author. Chapters are enriched by hymn verses and inspired original poetry.

The culmination of the journey is a prayer encouraging others to be blessed by the Christian Life found only through Salvation and Jesus Christ.

Marlowe R. Scott

Plentiful Harvest: Fertile Ground

Believing Without Seeing:
The Power of Faith
© 2015

SYNOPSIS:

Do you really need to see to believe?

The answer is "NO!"

The concept of faith is used in many ways, such as those we have faith in who we consider faithful family and friends. Also, objects such as cars and other material things may be thought of as faithful.

Is there something deeper connected to faith?

Believing Without Seeing: The Power of Faith addresses that question. Learn what it is and how to use the power of faith.

There is an addition about an abusive tongue included with this writing. It is destined to provoke thoughts and teach about harm caused by that little member of the human body.

Keeping It Real
The Straight and Narrow

MARLOWE R. SCOTT

Plentiful Harvest: Fertile Ground

Keeping It Real:
The Straight and Narrow
© 2016

SYNOPSIS:

With so many unreal and unfulfilling circumstances in our lives today, the spiritual nourishment found on the pages of *Keeping It Real: The Straight and Narrow* are more than encouraging.

There are certainly hindrances and temptations along life's journey. This story gives assurance that by believing in Jesus and following the message of Scripture, there is a definite reward for those who choose to press on.

To keep on the straight path—which is REAL—the author expresses the message through personal experiences, scriptures, hymns, and poetry—all of which point to her deep, personal walk with Jesus Christ. Her openness (coupled with honesty) are clearly evident, as well as her goal to inspire and make a positive impact in the lives of others.

Questions presented are meant to prompt personal evaluation of oneself to aid in keeping on the 'Straight and Narrow" as your personal journey unfolds.

Plentiful Harvest: Fertile Ground

Never Alone:
Intimate Times with Jesus
© 2017

SYNOPSIS:

The focus of seeking Jesus intimately and personally has benefits for every Christian. For the new Christian who may not have discovered this blessing, this book will lead the way.

Personal time with Him through prayer, scriptures, music, and poetry provide those qualities to not only grow closer to our Savior, but affords us the comfort found in applying these to our daily lives.

The author shares inspiration found in being alone by creatively applying and using God's creation, music, poetry, and scriptures demonstrating that even Jesus Christ sought times to be alone to pray, fellowship, and worship God.

Marlowe R. Scott

Plentiful Harvest: Fertile Ground

Worth the Journey:
The Train Ride to Glory
© 2016

SYNOPSIS:

This collection of three Amazon Best-Selling books inspirationally shares the author's personal spiritual growth while incorporating original poetry, scripture, and the telling of how life's experiences have blessed her. Through it all, she has remained focused on the promises of heavenly rewards and invites readers to join in the journey. It is made clear that journeying to Glory is worth every day God has allotted us.

Book #1 – Spiritual Growth: From Milk to Strong Meat highlights how the author has spiritually grown from early childhood to her present senior years as a Christian.

Book #2 – Believing Without Seeing: The Power of Faith clearly testifies to ways the Fruit of the Spirit has blessed biblical personalities, as well as the author. An eye-opening Addendum on the abusive tongue is enlightening and a must-read.

Book #3 – Keeping It Real: The Straight and Narrow continues the journey, still pointing to the Cross of Calvary. There are excellent poems and stories further inspiring others to join and complete the journey to Heaven.

Plentiful Harvest: Fertile Ground

"I AM" Cares:
His Eyes Are on the Sparrow
© 2018

SYNOPSIS:

How often have you considered your importance to God? If He watches over a little sparrow, be assured He will watch over you.

NO ONE is too insignificant to receive His divine love and protection through life's storms.

The message from the hymn "His Eye Is on the Sparrow" — plus scripture and poetry herein — confirm that this Great "I AM" cares!

Marlowe R. Scott
Owner/Creator

M.R.S. Inspirations
381 Lakehurst Road
Browns Mills, NJ 08015
Email: M.R.Boyce@att.net

"Specializing in Hand-Crafted Creations Giving Special Comfort and LOVE"

➢ Memory Pillows
➢ Memory Quilts
➢ Crib Quilts
➢ Throws
➢ And much, much more!

www.ingramcontent.com/pod-product-compliance
Lightning Source LLC
Chambersburg PA
CBHW052208110526
44591CB00012B/2133